SCHOOL YEAR _____

Doodle & Plan
Daily Planner for Teachers

THIS PLANNER BELONGS TO

_____

SCHOOL

_____

CLASSROOM #

_____

PHONE #

_____

Stephanie Ruiz Malone

My biggest desire is that you find this planner to be encouraging and fun to fill out as you progress through the academic year. I created a planner I wish I would have had as I started my journey as a teacher. It is my gift to you, my newest teacher friend. My hope is that it will make your planning sessions incredibly creative and productive.

****

You are wonderful and deserve the best things this world has to offer. You take on so many things on a daily basis. Don't be afraid to reach out for help when you really need it. Take a deep breath and know you are making a difference in this world. The light you spread reaches far beyond anything you could ever imagine. You are amazing!

I encourage you to read this message anytime you are having a stressful day.

****

Thank you so much for choosing this planner and letting me be a part of your teacher journey. This planner is also available in spiral-bound format through *lulu.com/shop* as an optional version for you. I value your honest review and look forward to hearing your thoughts. Subscribe to the Estrella Brillante newsletter for future product releases and year-round motivation and inspiration,
For easy access, scan the QR code below:
I have included a free mini motivational poster download for you

****

Created for you with ♡
Stephanie Ruiz Malone

Published by Stephanie Ruiz Malone
stephanieruizmalone.com

ISBN: 979-8-9882808-2-8

ISBN 979-8-9882808-2-8

9 798988 280828

Beginning-of-the-Year Notes

Have courage because teaching is worth the ride.

To-Do List

- [ ]
- [ ]
- [ ]
- [ ]
- [ ]
- [ ]
- [ ]
- [ ]
- [ ]
- [ ]
- [ ]
- [ ]
- [ ]
- [ ]
- [ ]
- [ ]
- [ ]
- [ ]
- [ ]
- [ ]
- [ ]
- [ ]
- [ ]
- [ ]
- [ ]
- [ ]

Faculty Meetings

Faculty Meetings

Every step builds upon another, don't forget to celebrate each one.

☺ Department Meetings

Department Meetings

Believe in yourself and your abilities.

Team Meetings

Team Meetings

Support your teacher friends because you are in this together.

District Meetings

District Meetings

Your voice is powerful!

Professional Development

Professional Development

Every moment as a teacher builds character.

Classroom Seating Chart

Classroom Seating Chart

Sensitive Student Information
(ALLERGIES, MEDICATION, SPED/504 INFO, ETC.)

Student	Details
_____	_____
_____	_____
_____	_____
_____	_____
_____	_____
_____	_____
_____	_____
_____	_____
_____	_____
_____	_____
_____	_____
_____	_____
_____	_____
_____	_____
_____	_____

Sensitive Student Information
(ALLERGIES, MEDICATION, SPED/504 INFO, ETC.)

Student

Details

_____   _____

_____   _____

_____   _____

_____   _____

_____   _____

_____   _____

_____   _____

_____   _____

_____   _____

_____   _____

_____   _____

_____   _____

_____   _____

_____   _____

_____   _____

Field Trips

Date:

Location:

Est. Departure time:

Est. Arrival time:

Items to bring:
-
-
-
-

Notes:

- - - - - - - - - - - - - -

Date:

Location:

Est. Departure time:

Est. Arrival time:

Items to bring:
-
-
-
-

Notes:

- - - - - - - - - - - - - -

Date:

Location:

Est. Departure time:

Est. Arrival time:

Items to bring:
-
-
-
-

Notes:

- - - - - - - - - - - - - -

Date:

Location:

Est. Departure time:

Est. Arrival time:

Items to bring:
-
-
-
-

Notes:

Doodles

August

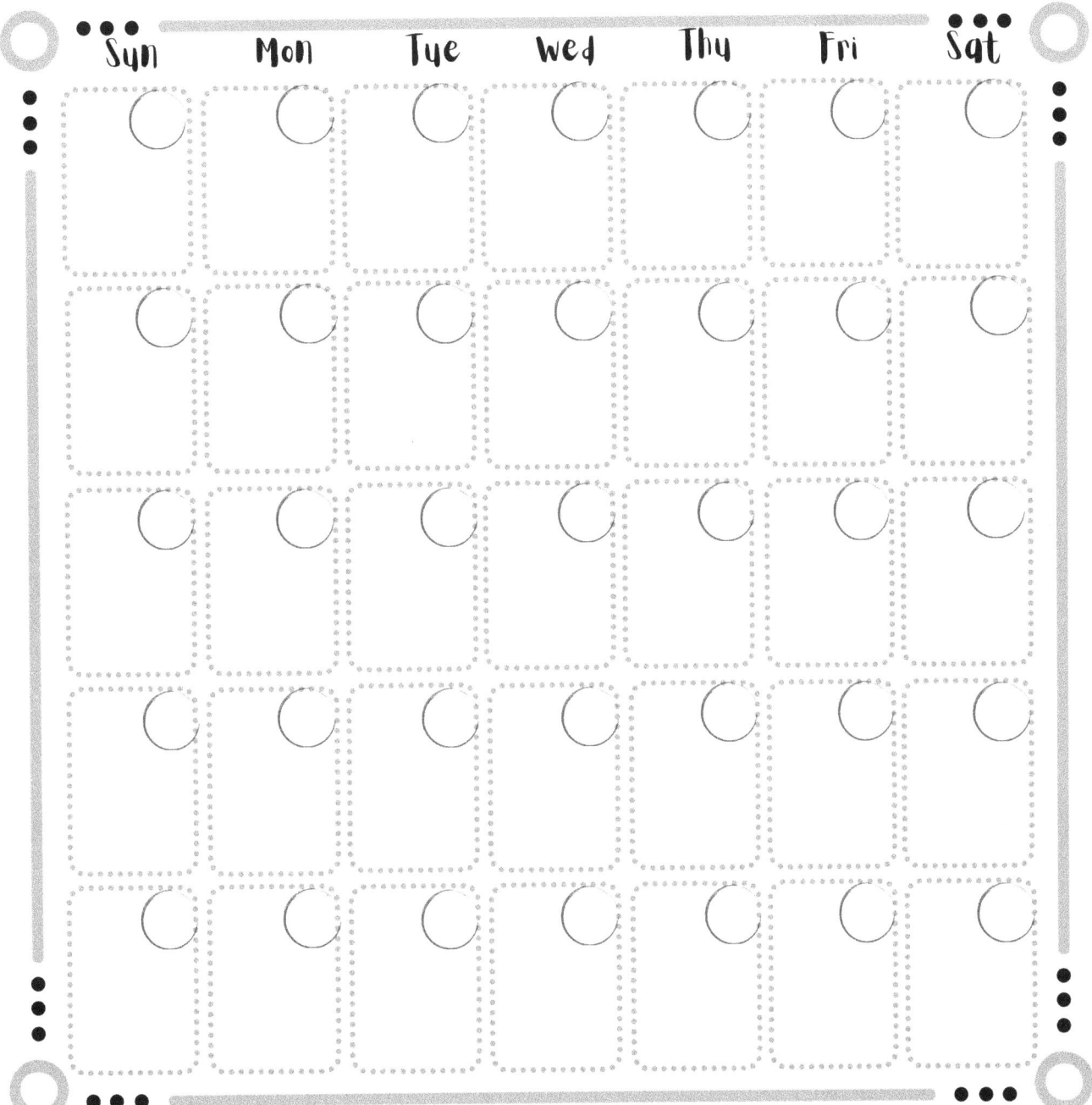

Sun	Mon	Tue	Wed	Thu	Fri	Sat

Birthdays:

Upcoming Events:

Week

Monday

● ● ● ● ● ● ● ● ● ● ● ● ● ●

Tuesday

● ● ● ● ● ● ● ● ● ● ● ● ● ●

Wednesday

● ● ● ● ● ● ● ● ● ● ● ● ● ●

Thursday

Friday

● ● ● ● ● ● ● ● ● ● ● ● ● ●

Calls/Emails

Supplies/Copies

Weekend

Week

Monday

Tuesday

Wednesday

Thursday

Friday

Supplies/Copies

Weekend

Calls/Emails

Week

Monday

• • • • • • • • • • • • • •

Tuesday

• • • • • • • • • • • • • •

Wednesday

• • • • • • • • • • • • • •

Thursday

• • • • • • • • • • • • • •

Friday

Calls/Emails

Supplies/Copies

Weekend

Calls/Emails

Week

Monday

Tuesday

Wednesday

Thursday

Friday

Supplies/Copies

Weekend

Week

Monday

Tuesday

Wednesday

Thursday

Friday

Calls/Emails

_____
_____
_____
_____
_____
_____
_____
_____
_____
_____
_____
_____

Supplies/Copies

_____
_____
_____
_____
_____
_____
_____
_____
_____
_____

Weekend

_____
_____
_____
_____
_____
_____
_____
_____
_____
_____

September

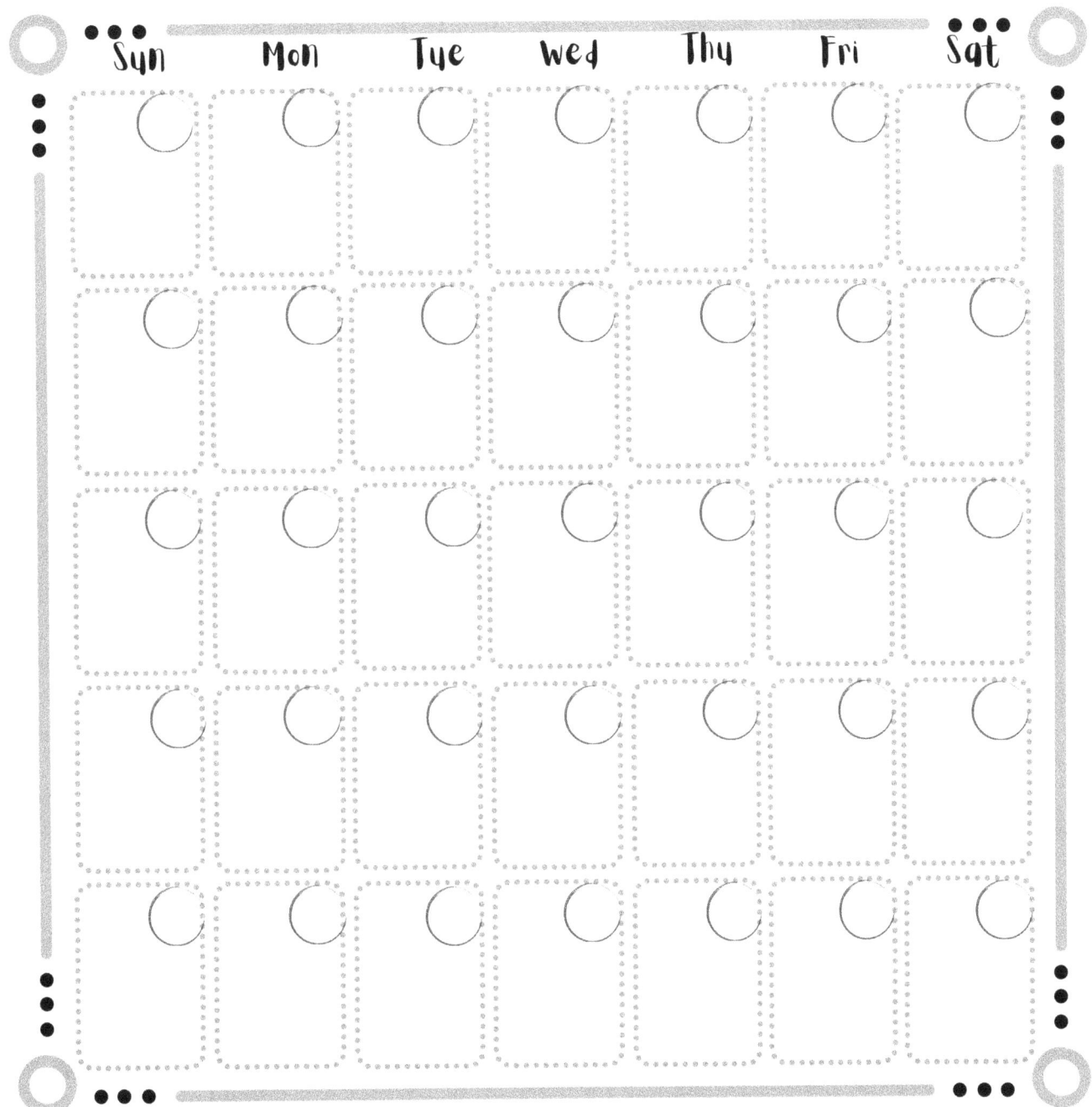

Sun	Mon	Tue	Wed	Thu	Fri	Sat

Birthdays:

Upcoming Events:

Week

Monday

• • • • • • • • • • • • • • •

Tuesday

Supplies/Copies

• • • • • • • • • • • • • • •

Wednesday

• • • • • • • • • • • • • • •

Thursday

Weekend

• • • • • • • • • • • • • • •

Friday

Calls/Emails

Week

Monday

Tuesday

Wednesday

Thursday

Friday

Supplies/Copies

Weekend

Week

Monday

• • • • • • • • • • • • •

Tuesday

• • • • • • • • • • • • •

Wednesday

• • • • • • • • • • • • •

Thursday

• • • • • • • • • • • • •

Friday

Calls/Emails

Supplies/Copies

Weekend

Calls/Emails

Week

Monday

● ● ● ● ● ● ● ● ● ● ● ● ● ● ●

Tuesday

● ● ● ● ● ● ● ● ● ● ● ● ● ● ●

Wednesday

● ● ● ● ● ● ● ● ● ● ● ● ● ● ●

Thursday

● ● ● ● ● ● ● ● ● ● ● ● ● ● ●

Friday

Calls/Emails

Supplies/Copies

Weekend

Week

Monday

Tuesday

Wednesday

Thursday

Friday

Supplies/Copies

Weekend

Calls/Emails

October

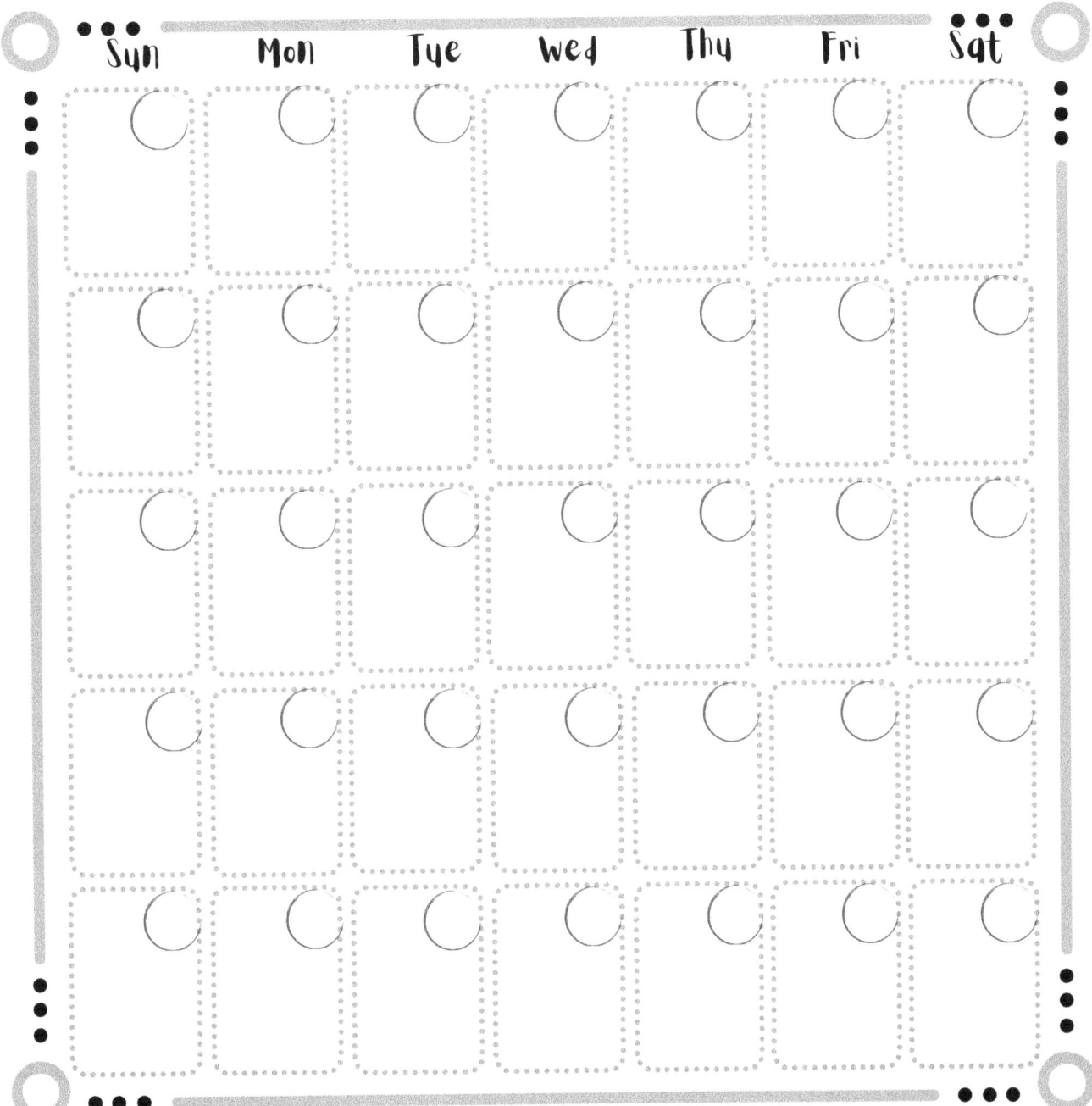

Sun	Mon	Tue	Wed	Thu	Fri	Sat

Birthdays:

Upcoming Events:

Week

Monday

● ● ● ● ● ● ● ● ● ● ● ● ● ● ●

Tuesday

● ● ● ● ● ● ● ● ● ● ● ● ● ● ●

Wednesday

● ● ● ● ● ● ● ● ● ● ● ● ● ● ●

Thursday

● ● ● ● ● ● ● ● ● ● ● ● ● ●

Friday

Calls/Emails

Supplies/Copies

Weekend

Week

Monday

Tuesday

Wednesday

Thursday

Friday

Week

Monday

• • • • • • • • • • • • • •

Tuesday

• • • • • • • • • • • • • •

Wednesday

• • • • • • • • • • • • • •

Thursday

• • • • • • • • • • • • • •

Friday

Calls/Emails

Supplies/Copies

Weekend

Calls/Emails

Week

Calls/Emails

Monday

- - - - - - - - - - - - - -
- - - - - - - - - - - - - -
- - - - - - - - - - - - - -
- - - - - - - - - - - - - -
- - - - - - - - - - - - - -
- - - - - - - - - - - - - -
- - - - - - - - - - - - - -
- - - - - - - - - - - - - -
- - - - - - - - - - - - - -
- - - - - - - - - - - - - -

Tuesday

• • • • • • • • • • • • • • • • •

Supplies/Copies

- - - - - - - - - - - - - -
- - - - - - - - - - - - - -
- - - - - - - - - - - - - -
- - - - - - - - - - - - - -
- - - - - - - - - - - - - -
- - - - - - - - - - - - - -
- - - - - - - - - - - - - -
- - - - - - - - - - - - - -

Wednesday

• • • • • • • • • • • • • • • • •

Thursday

Weekend

- - - - - - - - - - - - - -
- - - - - - - - - - - - - -
- - - - - - - - - - - - - -
- - - - - - - - - - - - - -
- - - - - - - - - - - - - -
- - - - - - - - - - - - - -
- - - - - - - - - - - - - -
- - - - - - - - - - - - - -

• • • • • • • • • • • • • • • • •

Friday

Week

Monday

• • • • • • • • • • • • • •

Tuesday

• • • • • • • • • • • • • •

Wednesday

• • • • • • • • • • • • • •

Thursday

• • • • • • • • • • • • • •

Friday

Calls/Emails

Supplies/Copies

Weekend

November

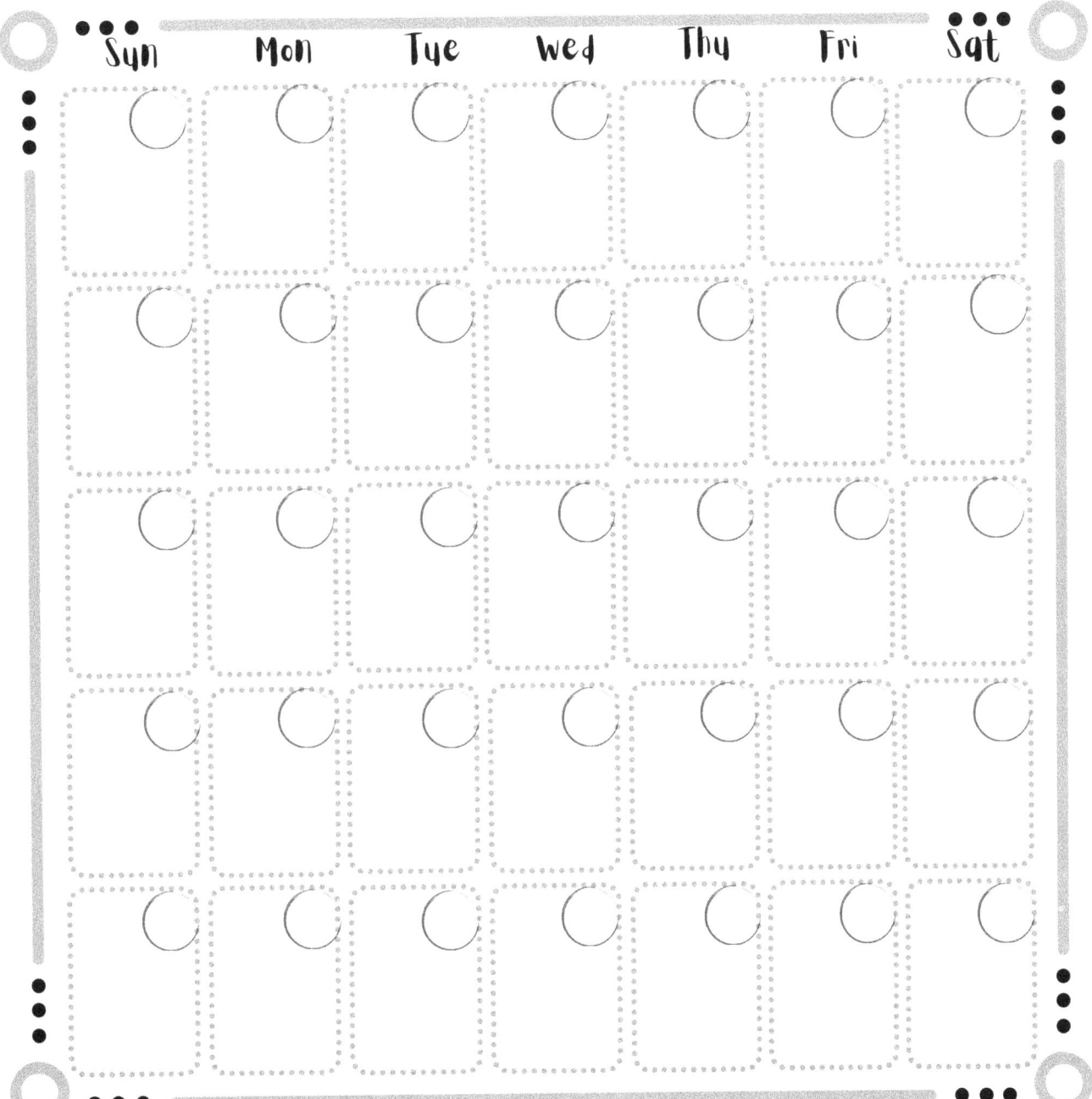

Sun	Mon	Tue	Wed	Thu	Fri	Sat

Birthdays:

Upcoming Events:

Week

Monday

• • • • • • • • • • • • • •

Tuesday

• • • • • • • • • • • • • • •

Wednesday

• • • • • • • • • • • • • • •

Thursday

• • • • • • • • • • • • • •

Friday

Calls/Emails

_____
_____
_____
_____
_____
_____
_____
_____
_____
_____
_____

Supplies/Copies

_____
_____
_____
_____
_____
_____
_____
_____
_____

Weekend

_____
_____
_____
_____
_____
_____
_____
_____
_____
_____

Calls/Emails

Week

Monday

Tuesday

Wednesday

Thursday

Friday

Supplies/Copies

Weekend

Week

Monday

• • • • • • • • • • • • • •

Tuesday

• • • • • • • • • • • • • •

Wednesday

• • • • • • • • • • • • • •

Thursday

Friday

• • • • • • • • • • • •

Calls/Emails

Supplies/Copies

Weekend

Week

Monday

Tuesday

Wednesday

Thursday

Friday

Calls/Emails

Supplies/Copies

Weekend

Week

Monday

Tuesday

Wednesday

Thursday

Friday

Calls/Emails

Supplies/Copies

Weekend

Calls/Emails

December

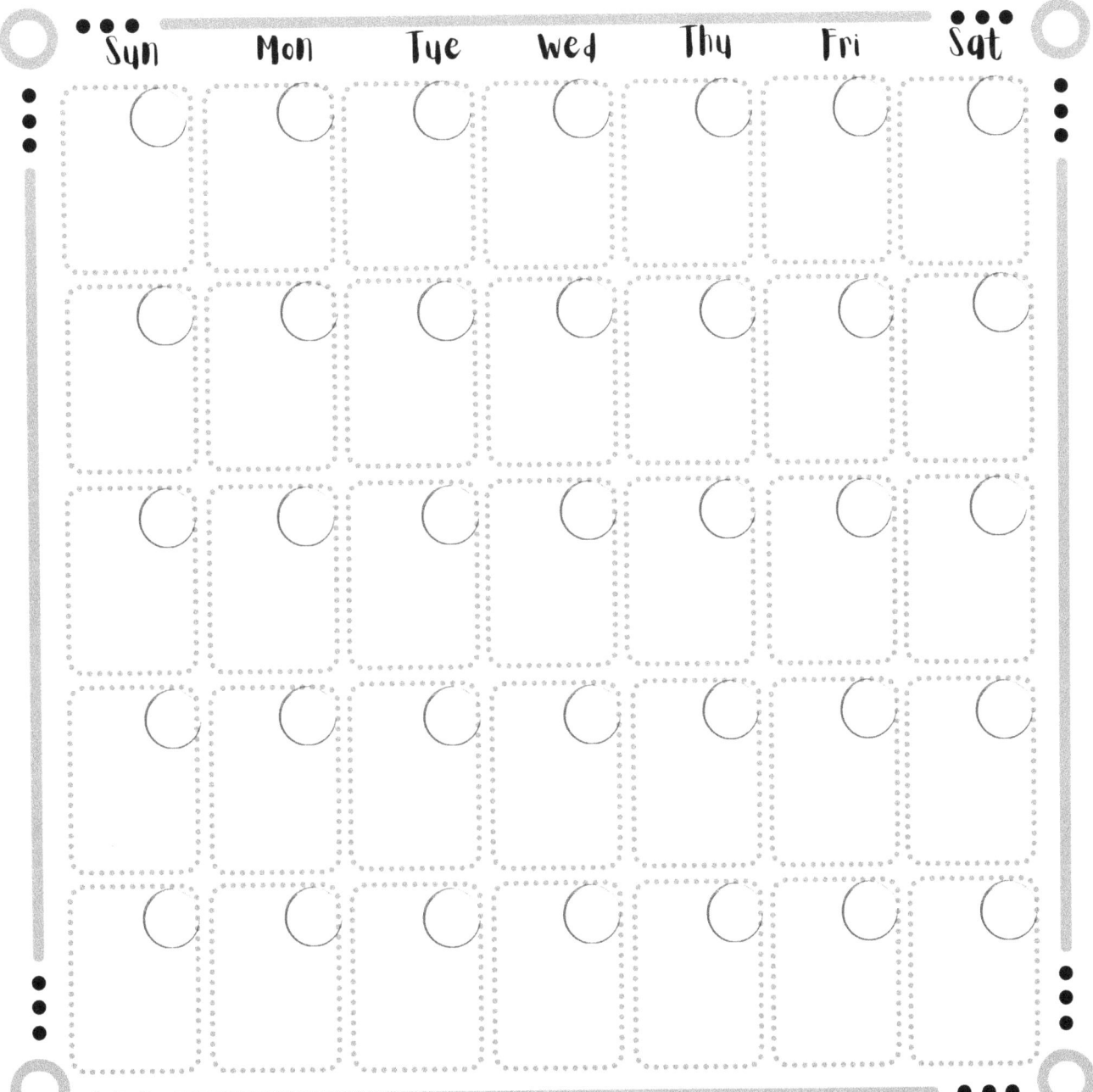

Sun	Mon	Tue	Wed	Thu	Fri	Sat

Birthdays:

Upcoming Events:

Week

Monday

• • • • • • • • • • • • • •

Tuesday

• • • • • • • • • • • • • •

Wednesday

• • • • • • • • • • • • • •

Thursday

• • • • • • • • • • • • • •

Friday

Calls/Emails

Supplies/Copies

Weekend

Week

Monday

Tuesday

Wednesday

Thursday

Friday

Calls/Emails

Supplies/Copies

Weekend

Week

Monday

- - - - - - - - - - - - - - - - -
- - - - - - - - - - - - - - - - -
- - - - - - - - - - - - - - - - -
- - - - - - - - - - - - - - - - -
- - - - - - - - - - - - - - - - -
- - - - - - - - - - - - - - - - -
- - - - - - - - - - - - - - - - -
- - - - - - - - - - - - - - - - -

• • • • • • • • • • • • • •

Tuesday

Supplies/Copies

- - - - - - - - - - - - - - - - -
- - - - - - - - - - - - - - - - -
- - - - - - - - - - - - - - - - -
- - - - - - - - - - - - - - - - -
- - - - - - - - - - - - - - - - -
- - - - - - - - - - - - - - - - -
- - - - - - - - - - - - - - - - -
- - - - - - - - - - - - - - - - -
- - - - - - - - - - - - - - - - -

• • • • • • • • • • • • • • •

Wednesday

• • • • • • • • • • • • • • • •

Thursday

Weekend

- - - - - - - - - - - - - - - - -
- - - - - - - - - - - - - - - - -
- - - - - - - - - - - - - - - - -
- - - - - - - - - - - - - - - - -
- - - - - - - - - - - - - - - - -
- - - - - - - - - - - - - - - - -
- - - - - - - - - - - - - - - - -
- - - - - - - - - - - - - - - - -
- - - - - - - - - - - - - - - - -
- - - - - - - - - - - - - - - - -

Calls/Emails

• • • • • • • • • • • • • •

Friday

Week

Monday

Tuesday

Wednesday

Thursday

Friday

Supplies/Copies

Weekend

Week

Monday

• • • • • • • • • • • • • • •

Tuesday

• • • • • • • • • • • • • • •

Wednesday

• • • • • • • • • • • • • • •

Thursday

• • • • • • • • • • • • • • •

Friday

Calls/Emails

Supplies/Copies

Weekend

Middle-of-the-Year Notes

Breathe though this challenging time, you've got this!

Classroom Seating Chart

Classroom Seating Chart

To-Do List

- [ ]
- [ ]
- [ ]
- [ ]
- [ ]
- [ ]
- [ ]
- [ ]
- [ ]
- [ ]
- [ ]
- [ ]
- [ ]
- [ ]
- [ ]
- [ ]
- [ ]
- [ ]
- [ ]
- [ ]
- [ ]
- [ ]
- [ ]
- [ ]
- [ ]
- [ ]

Doodles

Doodles

January

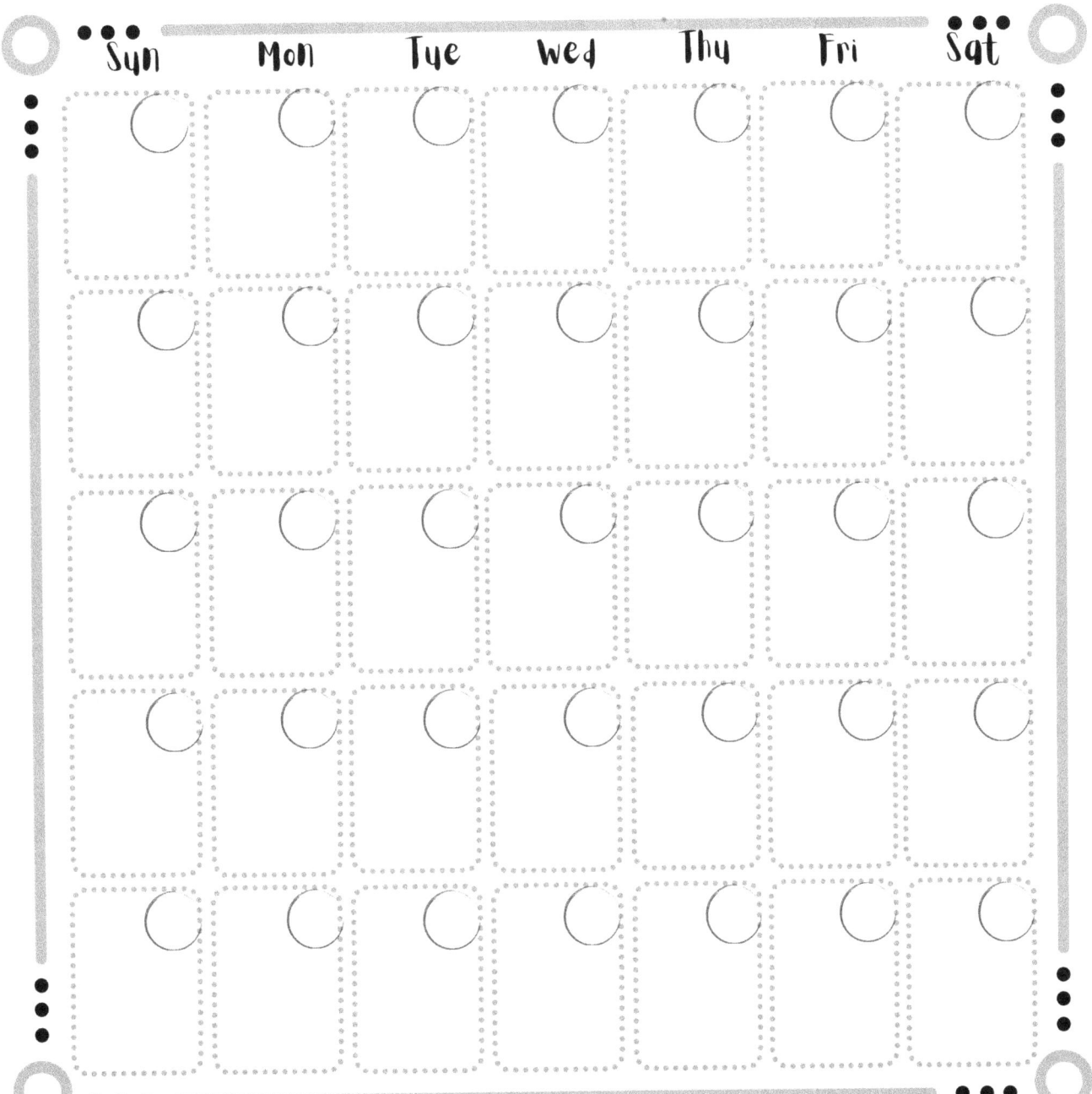

Sun	Mon	Tue	Wed	Thu	Fri	Sat

Birthdays:

Upcoming Events:

Week

Monday

• • • • • • • • • • • • • • • •

Tuesday

• • • • • • • • • • • • • • • •

Wednesday

• • • • • • • • • • • • • • • •

Thursday

• • • • • • • • • • • • • • • •

Friday

Calls/Emails

Supplies/Copies

Weekend

Week

Monday

Tuesday

Wednesday

Thursday

Friday

Supplies / Copies

Weekend

Week

Monday

Tuesday

Supplies/Copies

Wednesday

Thursday

Weekend

Friday

Calls/Emails

Week

Monday

●●●●●●●●●●●●●●●●●

Tuesday

●●●●●●●●●●●●●●●●●

Wednesday

●●●●●●●●●●●●●●●●●

Thursday

Friday

●●●●●●●●●●●●●●●●●

Calls/Emails

Supplies/Copies

Weekend

Week

Monday

⬤ ⬤ ⬤ ⬤ ⬤ ⬤ ⬤ ⬤ ⬤ ⬤ ⬤ ⬤ ⬤ ⬤

- - - - - - - - - - - - - - -
- - - - - - - - - - - - - - -
- - - - - - - - - - - - - - -
- - - - - - - - - - - - - - -
- - - - - - - - - - - - - - -
- - - - - - - - - - - - - - -
- - - - - - - - - - - - - - -
- - - - - - - - - - - - - - -
- - - - - - - - - - - - - - -
- - - - - - - - - - - - - - -

Tuesday

⬤ ⬤ ⬤ ⬤ ⬤ ⬤ ⬤ ⬤ ⬤ ⬤ ⬤ ⬤ ⬤ ⬤

Supplies / Copies

- - - - - - - - - - - - - - -
- - - - - - - - - - - - - - -
- - - - - - - - - - - - - - -
- - - - - - - - - - - - - - -
- - - - - - - - - - - - - - -
- - - - - - - - - - - - - - -
- - - - - - - - - - - - - - -
- - - - - - - - - - - - - - -
- - - - - - - - - - - - - - -
- - - - - - - - - - - - - - -

Wednesday

⬤ ⬤ ⬤ ⬤ ⬤ ⬤ ⬤ ⬤ ⬤ ⬤ ⬤ ⬤ ⬤ ⬤

Thursday

Weekend

- - - - - - - - - - - - - - -
- - - - - - - - - - - - - - -
- - - - - - - - - - - - - - -
- - - - - - - - - - - - - - -
- - - - - - - - - - - - - - -

⬤ ⬤ ⬤ ⬤ ⬤ ⬤ ⬤ ⬤ ⬤ ⬤ ⬤ ⬤ ⬤

- - - - - - - - - - - - - - -
- - - - - - - - - - - - - - -
- - - - - - - - - - - - - - -
- - - - - - - - - - - - - - -

Friday

February

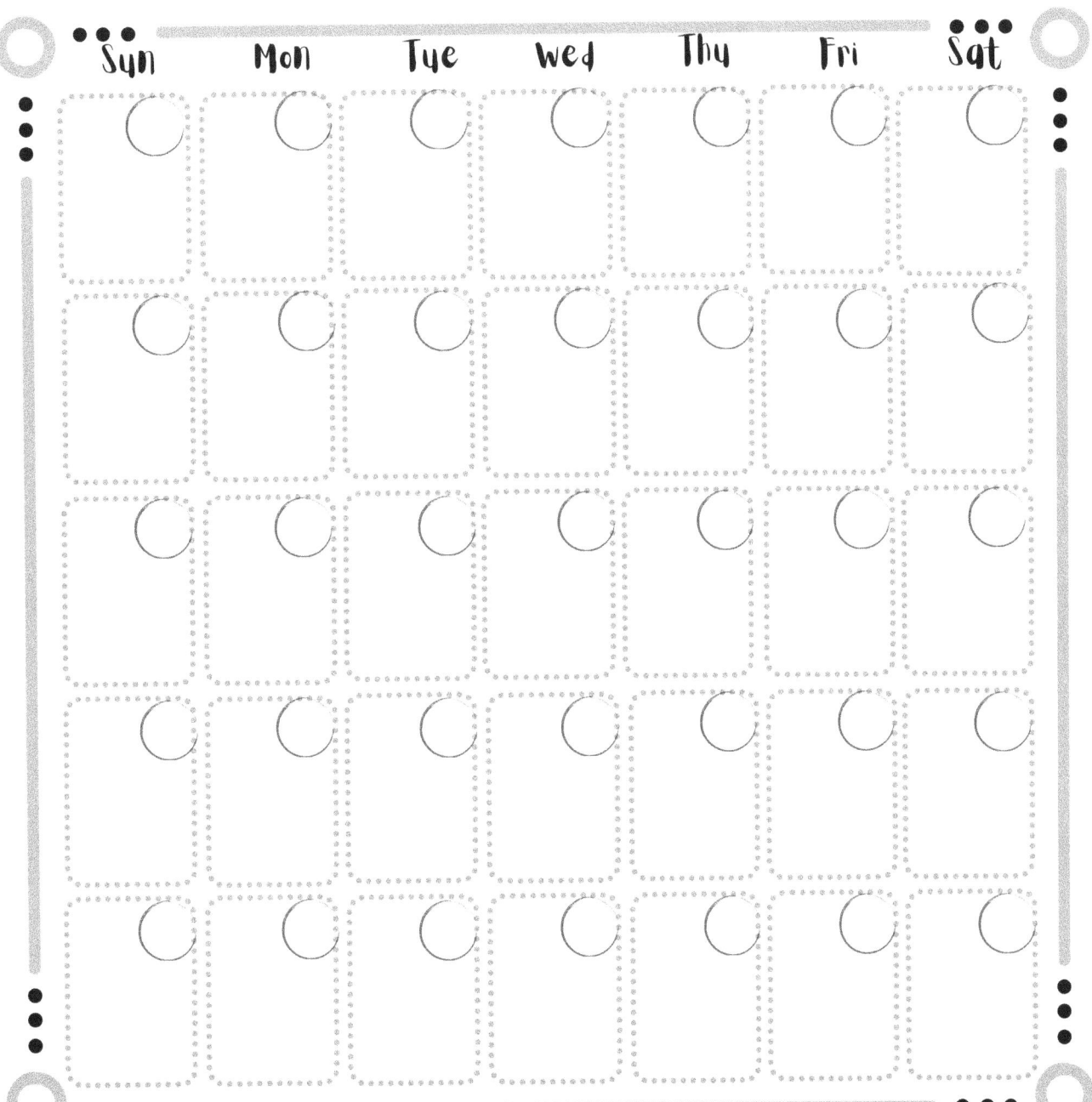

Sun	Mon	Tue	Wed	Thu	Fri	Sat

Birthdays:

Upcoming Events:

Week

Monday

Tuesday

Wednesday

Thursday

Friday

Supplies/Copies

Weekend

Calls/Emails

Week

Monday

Tuesday

Wednesday

Thursday

Friday

Calls/Emails

Supplies/Copies

Weekend

Week

Monday

• • • • • • • • • • • • • •

Tuesday

• • • • • • • • • • • • • •

Wednesday

• • • • • • • • • • • • • •

Thursday

• • • • • • • • • • • • • •

Friday

Calls/Emails

Supplies/Copies

Weekend

Calls/Emails

Week

Monday

Tuesday

Wednesday

Thursday

Friday

Week

Monday

• • • • • • • • • • • • • • • •

Tuesday

• • • • • • • • • • • • • • • •

Wednesday

• • • • • • • • • • • • • • • •

Thursday

• • • • • • • • • • • • • • • •

Friday

Calls/Emails

Supplies/Copies

Weekend

Calls/Emails

March

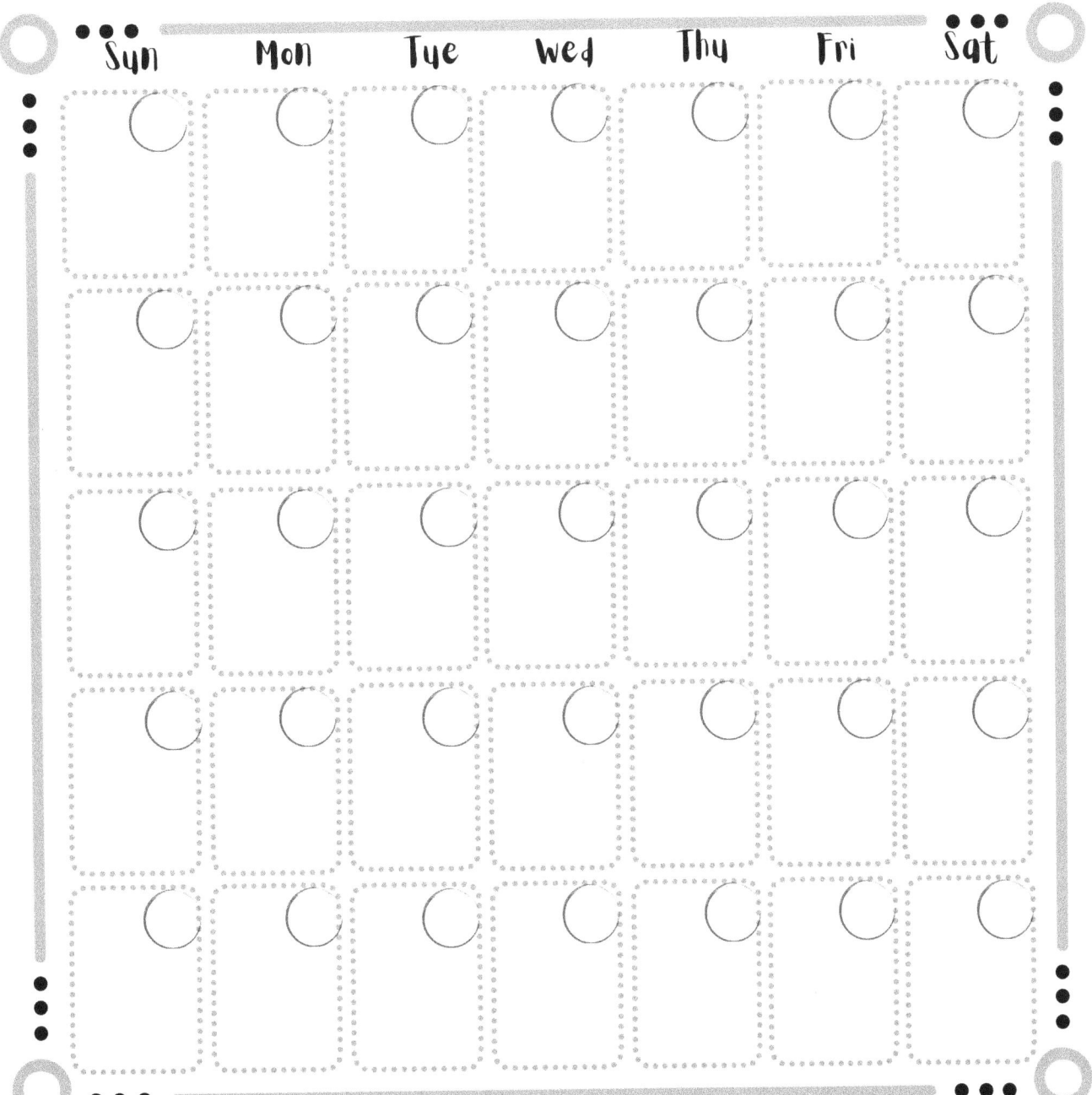

Sun	Mon	Tue	Wed	Thu	Fri	Sat

Birthdays:

Upcoming Events:

Week

Monday

● ● ● ● ● ● ● ● ● ● ● ● ● ● ●

Tuesday

● ● ● ● ● ● ● ● ● ● ● ● ● ● ●

Wednesday

● ● ● ● ● ● ● ● ● ● ● ● ● ● ●

Thursday

● ● ● ● ● ● ● ● ● ● ● ● ● ● ●

Friday

Calls/Emails

Supplies/Copies

Weekend

Calls/Emails

Week

Monday

Tuesday

Wednesday

Thursday

Friday

Calls / Emails

Supplies / Copies

Weekend

Week

Monday

Tuesday

Wednesday

Thursday

Friday

Supplies / Copies

Weekend

Calls / Emails

Week

Monday

Tuesday

Wednesday

Thursday

Friday

Calls/Emails

Supplies/Copies

Weekend

Calls/Emails

Week

Monday

Tuesday

Wednesday

Thursday

Friday

Calls/Emails

Supplies/Copies

Weekend

April

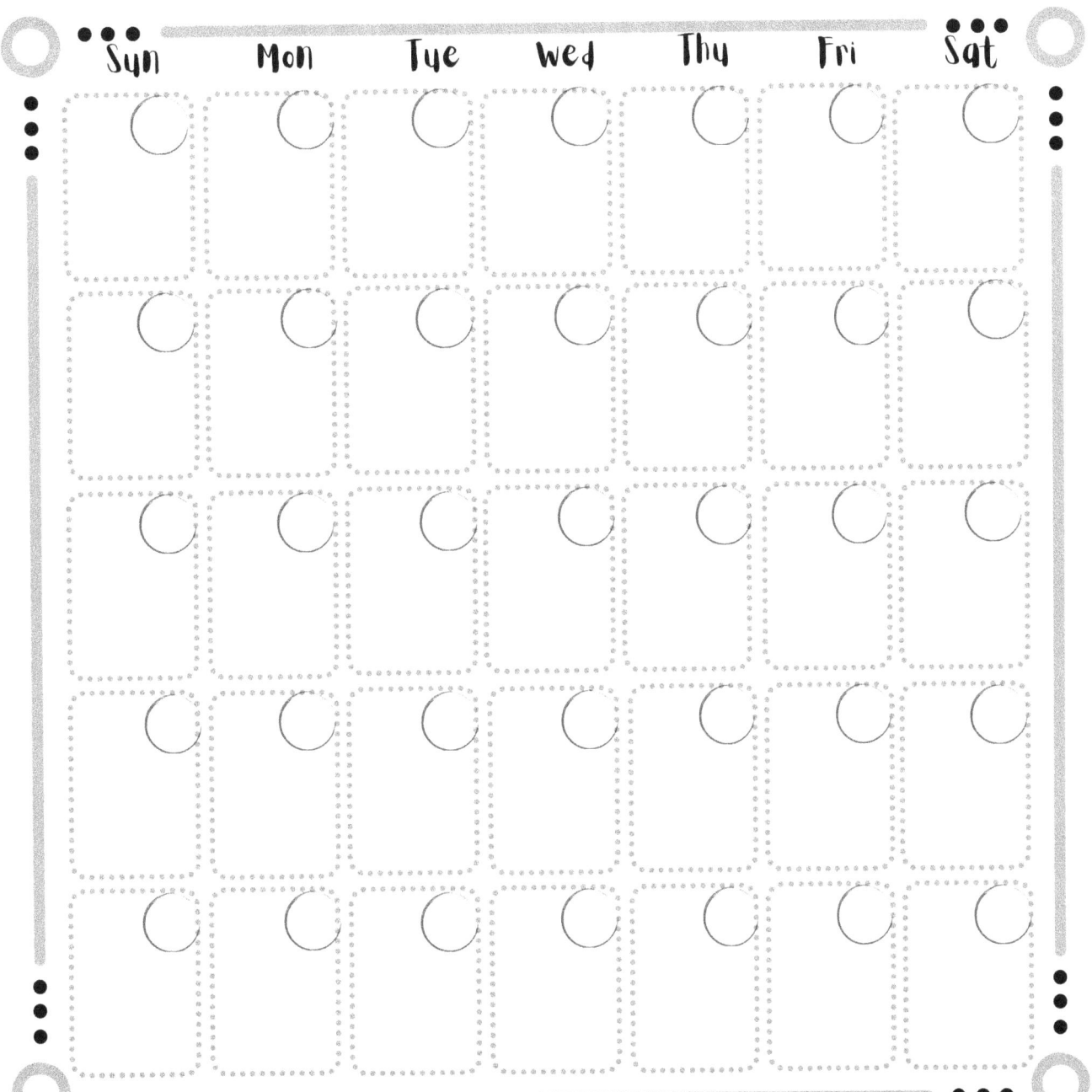

Sun	Mon	Tue	Wed	Thu	Fri	Sat

Birthdays:

Upcoming Events:

Week

Monday

Tuesday

Wednesday

Thursday

Friday

Calls/Emails

Supplies/Copies

Weekend

Week

Monday

• • • • • • • • • • • • • • • • •

Tuesday

• • • • • • • • • • • • • • • • •

Wednesday

• • • • • • • • • • • • • • • • •

Thursday

Friday

• • • • • • • • • • • • • • • • •

Calls/Emails

Supplies/Copies

Weekend

Calls/Emails

Week

Monday

Tuesday

Wednesday

Thursday

Friday

Supplies/Copies

Weekend

Week

Monday

Tuesday

Wednesday

Thursday

Friday

Calls / Emails

Supplies / Copies

Weekend

Calls / Emails

Week

Monday

Tuesday

Wednesday

Supplies/Copies

Thursday

Weekend

Friday

Calls/Emails

May

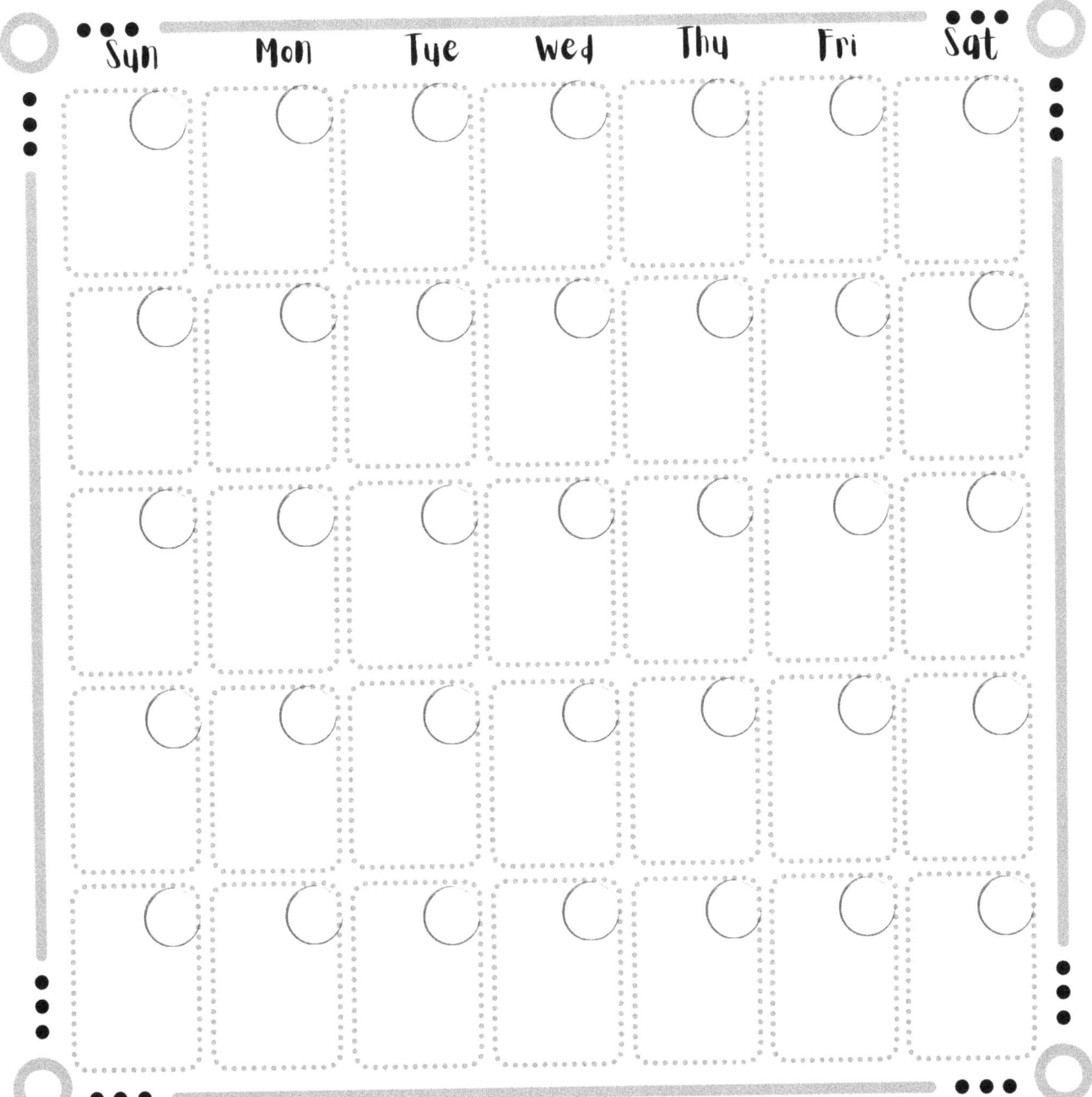

Sun	Mon	Tue	Wed	Thu	Fri	Sat

Birthdays:

Upcoming Events:

Week

Monday

Tuesday

Wednesday

Thursday

Friday

Calls/Emails

Supplies/Copies

Weekend

Week

Monday

Tuesday

Wednesday

Thursday

Friday

Calls / Emails
_____
_____
_____
_____
_____
_____
_____
_____
_____

Supplies / Copies
_____
_____
_____
_____
_____
_____
_____
_____

Weekend
_____
_____
_____
_____
_____
_____
_____
_____
_____

Week

Monday

· · · · · · · · · · · · · · ·

Tuesday

Supplies/Copies

· · · · · · · · · · · · · · ·

Wednesday

· · · · · · · · · · · · · · ·

Thursday

Weekend

· · · · · · · · · · · · · · ·

Friday

Week

Monday

Tuesday

Wednesday

Thursday

Friday

Calls / Emails

Supplies / Copies

Weekend

Week

Monday

Tuesday

Wednesday

Thursday

Friday

Calls/Emails

Supplies/Copies

Weekend

June

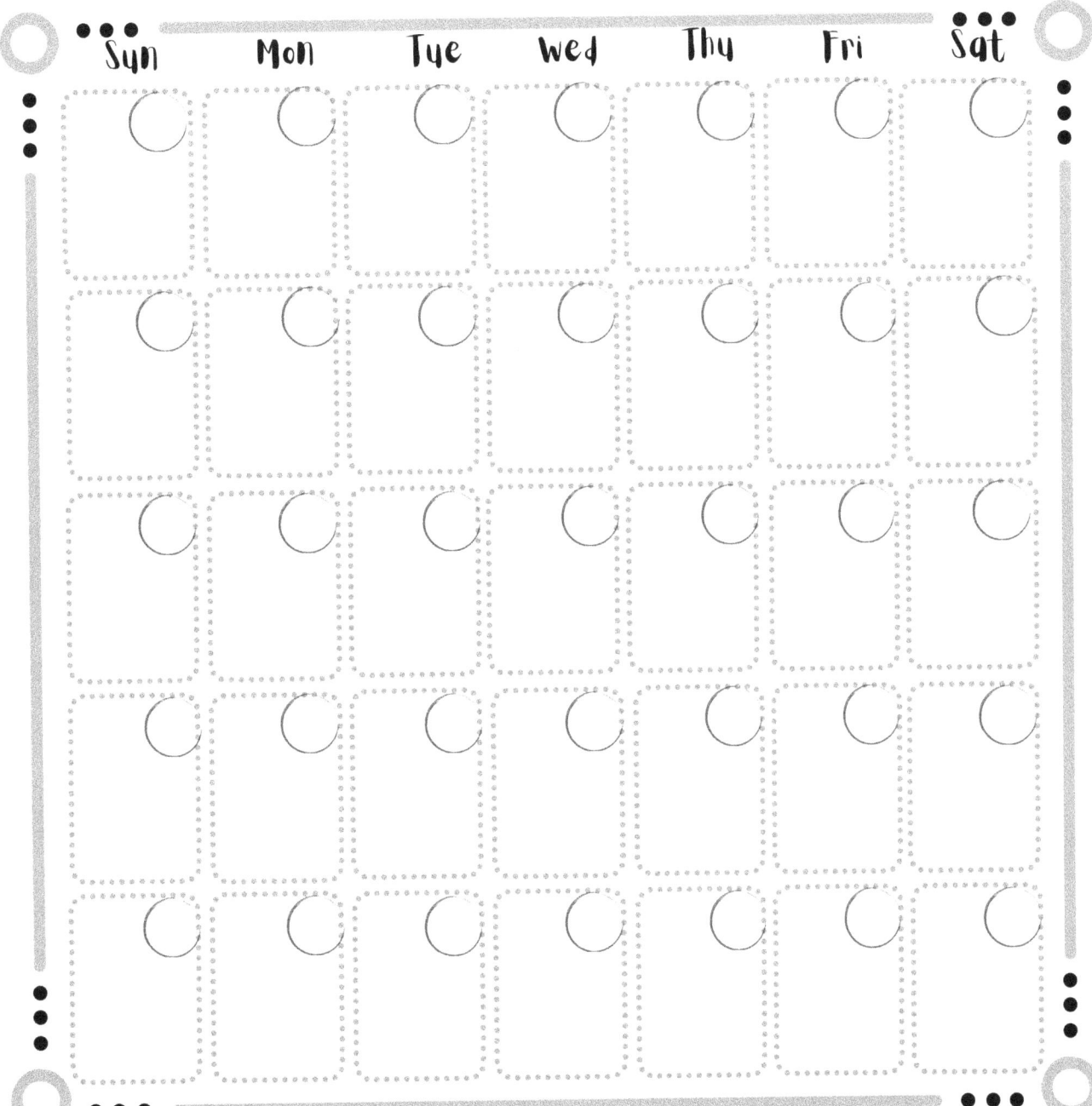

Sun	Mon	Tue	Wed	Thu	Fri	Sat

Birthdays: Upcoming Events:

Week

Monday

• • • • • • • • • • • • • • •

Tuesday

• • • • • • • • • • • • • • •

Wednesday

• • • • • • • • • • • • • • •

Thursday

• • • • • • • • • • • • • • •

Friday

Calls/Emails

Supplies/Copies

Weekend

Calls/Emails

Week

Monday

● ● ● ● ● ● ● ● ● ● ● ● ● ● ●

Tuesday

● ● ● ● ● ● ● ● ● ● ● ● ● ● ●

Supplies/Copies

Wednesday

● ● ● ● ● ● ● ● ● ● ● ● ● ● ●

Thursday

Weekend

● ● ● ● ● ● ● ● ● ● ● ● ● ● ●

Friday

Calls/Emails

Week

Monday

• • • • • • • • • • • • • • •

Tuesday

• • • • • • • • • • • • • • •

Supplies / Copies

Wednesday

• • • • • • • • • • • • • • •

Thursday

Weekend

• • • • • • • • • • • • • • •

Friday

Calls / Emails

Week

Monday

• • • • • • • • • • • • • • • • •

Tuesday

• • • • • • • • • • • • • • • • •

Wednesday

• • • • • • • • • • • • • • • • •

Thursday

Friday

• • • • • • • • • • • • • • • • •

Calls/Emails

_____
_____
_____
_____
_____
_____
_____
_____
_____
_____

Supplies/Copies

_____
_____
_____
_____
_____
_____
_____
_____
_____

Weekend

_____
_____
_____
_____
_____
_____
_____
_____
_____

Week

Monday

● ● ● ● ● ● ● ● ● ● ● ● ● ●

Tuesday

Supplies / Copies

● ● ● ● ● ● ● ● ● ● ● ● ● ●

Wednesday

● ● ● ● ● ● ● ● ● ● ● ● ● ●

Thursday

Weekend

● ● ● ● ● ● ● ● ● ● ● ● ●

Friday

Calls / Emails

End-of-the-Year Notes ☀

Rest, replenish, and reflect.

To-Do List

- [ ]
- [ ]
- [ ]
- [ ]
- [ ]
- [ ]
- [ ]
- [ ]
- [ ]
- [ ]
- [ ]
- [ ]
- [ ]
- [ ]
- [ ]
- [ ]
- [ ]
- [ ]
- [ ]
- [ ]
- [ ]
- [ ]
- [ ]
- [ ]
- [ ]
- [ ]

July

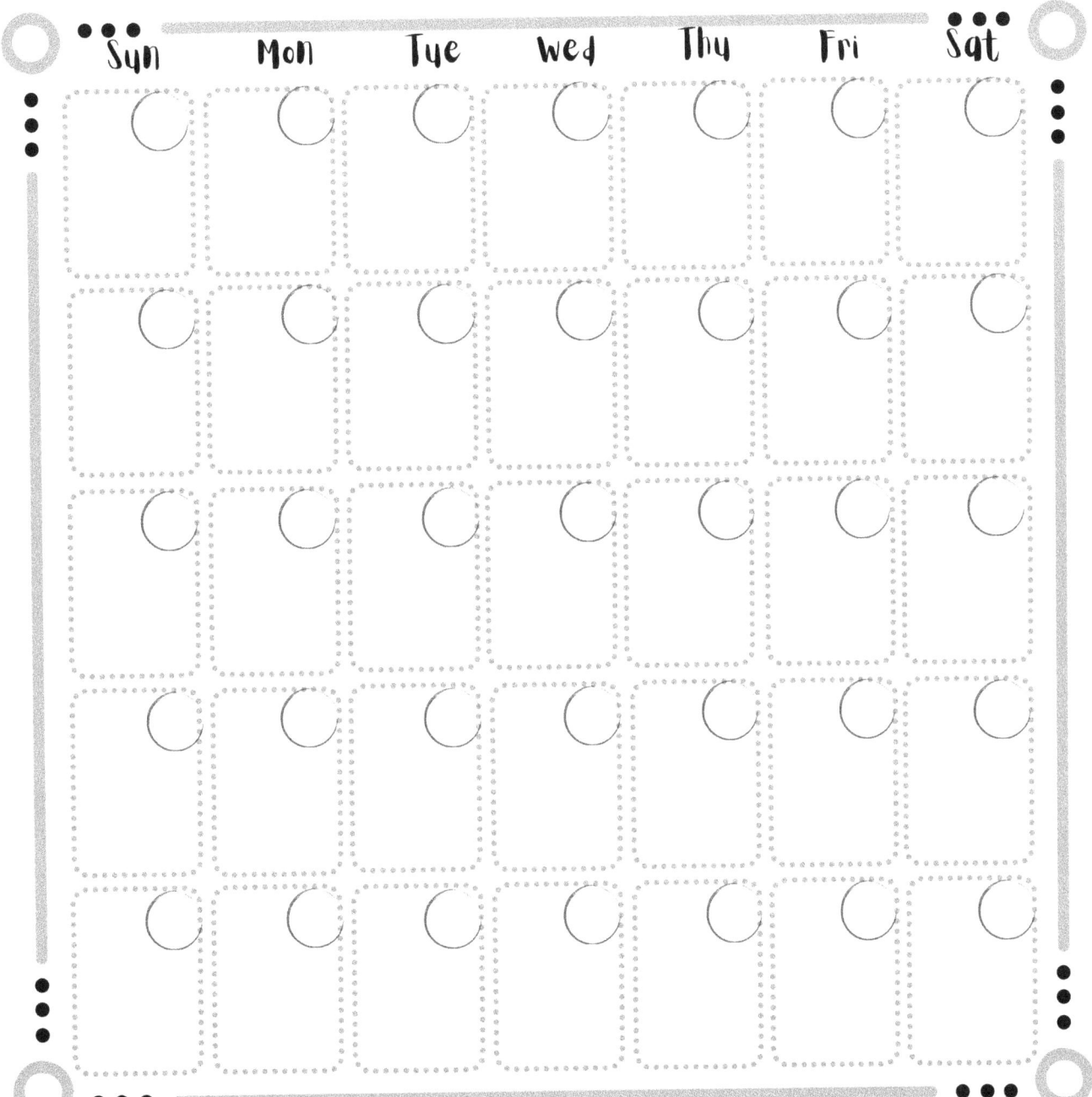

Sun	Mon	Tue	Wed	Thu	Fri	Sat

Birthdays:

Upcoming Events:

Week

Monday

• • • • • • • • • • • • • • • •

Tuesday

• • • • • • • • • • • • • • • •

Wednesday

• • • • • • • • • • • • • • • •

Thursday

• • • • • • • • • • • • • • • •

Friday

Calls/Emails

Supplies/Copies

Weekend

Week

Monday

Tuesday

Wednesday

Thursday

Friday

Calls/Emails

Supplies/Copies

Weekend

Calls/Emails

Week

Monday

Tuesday

Wednesday

Thursday

Friday

Supplies/Copies

Weekend

Week

Monday

• • • • • • • • • • • • • • • •

Tuesday

Supplies/Copies

• • • • • • • • • • • • • • • •

Wednesday

• • • • • • • • • • • • • • • •

Thursday

Weekend

• • • • • • • • • • • • • • • •

Friday

Week

Monday

• • • • • • • • • • • • • •

Tuesday

• • • • • • • • • • • • • •

Wednesday

• • • • • • • • • • • • • •

Thursday

• • • • • • • • • • • • • •

Friday

Calls/Emails

Supplies/Copies

Weekend

Calls/Emails

Doodles

Website Login Info.

website:
username:
password:
notes:

website:
username:
password:
notes:

website:
username:
password:
notes:

website:
username:
password:
notes:

website:
username:
password:
notes:

website:
username:
password:
notes:

website:
username:
password:
notes:

website:
username:
password:
notes:

website:
username:
password:
notes:

website:
username:
password:
notes:

website:
username:
password:
notes:

website:
username:
password:
notes:

Quick Parent Contact Notes

Date: Student: Action Plan:

Strengths: Concerns:

- O   O
- O   O
- O   O

....

Date: Student: Action Plan:

Strengths: Concerns:

- O   O
- O   O
- O   O

....

Date: Student: Action Plan:

Strengths: Concerns:

- O   O
- O   O
- O   O

....

Date: Student: Action Plan:

Strengths: Concerns:

- O   O
- O   O
- O   O

Quick Parent Contact Notes

Date: Student: Action Plan:
Strengths: Concerns:

O O

O O

O O

Date: Student: Action Plan:
Strengths: Concerns:

O O

O O

O O

Date: Student: Action Plan:
Strengths: Concerns:

O O

O O

O O

Date: Student: Action Plan:
Strengths: Concerns:

O O

O O

O O

Quick Parent Contact Notes

Date: Student: Action Plan:

Strengths: Concerns:

- ○
- ○
- ○

          ○
          ○
          ○

- -

Date: Student: Action Plan:

Strengths: Concerns:

- ○
- ○
- ○

          ○
          ○
          ○

- -

Date: Student: Action Plan:

Strengths: Concerns:

- ○
- ○
- ○

          ○
          ○
          ○

- -

Date: Student: Action Plan:

Strengths: Concerns:

- ○
- ○
- ○

          ○
          ○
          ○

Quick Parent Contact Notes

Date: Student: Action Plan:

Strengths: Concerns:

- ○
- ○
- ○

     ○
     ○
     ○

Date: Student: Action Plan:

Strengths: Concerns:

- ○
- ○
- ○

     ○
     ○
     ○

Date: Student: Action Plan:

Strengths: Concerns:

- ○
- ○
- ○

     ○
     ○
     ○

Date: Student: Action Plan:

Strengths: Concerns:

- ○
- ○
- ○

     ○
     ○
     ○

Quick Parent Contact Notes

Date: Student: Action Plan:
Strengths: Concerns:

O   O

O   O

O   O

- -

Date: Student: Action Plan:
Strengths: Concerns:

O   O

O   O

O   O

- -

Date: Student: Action Plan:
Strengths: Concerns:

O   O

O   O

O   O

- -

Date: Student: Action Plan:
Strengths: Concerns:

O   O

O   O

O   O

Reflections

 Doodles